Julian Turner · Desolate Market

Julian Turner has published three previous collections of poetry: *Crossing the Outskirts*, a Poetry Book Society Recommendation which was shortlisted for the Forward Prize best first collection in 2002, *Orphan Sites* (2006) and *Planet-Struck* (2011). Born in Cheadle Hulme, near Manchester, in 1955, he was educated at New College, Oxford and Goldsmiths, London. From 2013–15 he was Royal Literary Fund Fellow at Leeds University. He lives with his partner in Otley, West Yorkshire, and works as a writer and counsellor.

ALSO BY JULIAN TURNER

Crossing the Outskirts
(2002)

Orphan Sites
(2006)

Planet-Struck
(2011)

Julian Turner

Desolate Market

CARCANET

First published in Great Britain in 2018 by

Carcanet Press Limited
Alliance House
Cross Street
Manchester M2 7AQ
www.carcanet.co.uk

We welcome your feedback: info@carcanet.co.uk

A CIP catalogue record for this book is available
from the British Library, ISBN 978 1 784105 12 9

The publisher acknowledges financial assistance
from Arts Council England

Set in Monotype Dante by Anvil
Printed and bound in England by SRP Ltd, Exeter

Wisdom is sold in the desolate market
where none come to buy.

WILLIAM BLAKE
Vela, or the Four Zoas

ACKNOWLEDGEMENTS

Some of these poems have appeared in the following publications:

'Yorkshire Giant' in *13 Pages*; 'A Man' and 'Care' in *Versions of the North,* ed. Ian Parks, Five Leaves Press; 'The Old Camel' and 'The Rhubarb Triangle' in *Stand*; 'A Separation' in *The Honest Ulsterman*; the 'Black Box' section in *Poetry Review*.

Contents

3 DESOLATE MARKET

4 SILENT VACUUM

I
Place-Time

Lairig Ghru

A river pours out of a pile of stones.

We stand at the head of the pass and watch
the desolation. Something stirs
behind the granite face, the ling.
The rocks are ancient, cold. They set
in frowns and turn their backs on me
or stand above me, lowering.

The high peaks are the sentinels.
They have their own agenda none
can read. Their heads are always
in the clouds, their minds have wandered,
are misguided and perverse.
They have got it in for me.

The prospect is alarming – I
am suddenly sick of the sight of it:
the way the rock-teeth pierce the snow,
the drone and sobs of a sore wind
that whines across the moors and drowns
the isolated hums of life.

I am afraid of everything:
100-year-old snow, lifeless rocks,
vistas without limit. I cannot
even recognise my brother
who drifts like smoke across the pass
between the mountains and the clouds.

Let me get the fuck out.

Windfall

Autumn is speech in the mouth of the dead,
bronchitis in the lungs of trees
coughing down conkers
on the roads by London Fields,
a vertical transhumance of souls.
Their coals incandesce on the tarmac,
as bronze as whiskey
gloved by winceyette
peeping from fists of spikes.

I scoop them overflowing
in my hands,
pouring over my sleeves,
liquid rosewood.
My skin is onion paper
over early drafts of veins,
see-through in sharp light, ghostly
as air that dances over burning leaves.
I'm almost dead

and am collecting them for you
like relics to remind you of autumn.
They live in my arms
and everything I do is imaginary:
inhaling ground-frost,
the cousinly hand of the wind in my hair
and gathering these hearts,
still warm,
for your fingers to wonder at.

Yorkshire Giant

Ill-considered from scratch, it still has grace –
a slope of maple, oak and forget-me-not
by a C-road on the Chevin, a nameless place
where old carpets and broken branches rot,
where people dump empty Budweiser bottles,
black bin-bags spilling yellow Fosters tins
or building-rubble under stained tarpaulins,
a desecrated space watched over by immortals:

the giant Jack-in-Irons, whose dripping chains
clank as he walks the empty roads by dark
in search of people and their secret stains,
who knows you and your sort, stands rooted
to the Earth with one foot planted here
in this copse, his rainbow-paned face a hundred
feet above tumbling warnings of the lark,
turning his legendary head so he can hear.

Jodrell Bank

A little bit of heaven crouching there,
its skeleton a sketch of nebulae,
its hemisphere collecting breath of stars,
our dreams beamed down in ways we can receive
like dust that gathered on the pantry shelves
from nowhere and was such a mystery.

The dish was only down the road from school,
a hop from Alderley, unreachable
to me, though once my Dad drove us inside
and let us touch the girders of the wheel.
Since then I've felt connected to the rule
of unseen frequencies that are my guide.

It stood for so much more than I could see,
a spectrum of the infinite and this
ungainly structure opened up arcane
wavelengths, doors in the dark sky, sent me
the soft intangibles of mimesis,
a metal flower on the Cheshire plain.

Everything Keeps Turning to Water

The space of the sky suspended over us as we creep
    across the causeway into a headwind,
the black clouds massed behind us among Hecla and
    Beinn Mhor,
the rush of the tides in the creeks at the edge of the
    islands which merge into freshwater lochans on
    paper-thin land,
the roar in our ears as we crawl up over the moors on
    the broad back of the north island;

I can keep it at bay as I ride into the cold wind, barely
    making headway, having to pedal hard downhill
    in the chill, thick cloud clamped over Clisham,
but when I stop and the gneiss stretches on forever
    around me grinding the greywacke of the clouds
making grain of us, then the solid world begins to
    shiver and shake.

The white water round the skerries, rough with the
    wash of wind and tide, the shoreline and the open
    hand of sea,
the sky's surface with its rafts of cloud, its dark,
    shadowy skeins of rain, the one white fingernail
    of sand in the purple dusk
and even though it does not matter at all, every outline
    and colour turns invariably into water.

The sepia morass, a blanket stretched across the whole
    mass of Lewis, steeped in perpetual souse of rain,
the arrow of the road leading on into the North, rising
    and dipping over endless waves of dripping peat,

the ruins cataloguing the roadside, the lack of anywhere
warm or dry to sit, everywhere that was ever open
shut now, left alone and cold,
the stub of the lighthouse in the distance, a tiny signal
so insignificant that it can barely be discerned.

I have been in love all my life with someone I no longer
recognise.

Mingulay

for Rainier and Johanna Salverda

Immense and blank and close enough to touch,
their bed-on-bed of metamorphic rock
glistening black and veined with red feldspar,

the two hundred metre cliffs of Mingulay
rise and fall with each swell of twenty foot
as we drift between the island and the stack

where elements contend and play their game
of scissors, paper, stone: sea eats out rock,
rocks cut the wind and wind frenzies the sea.

Now the cliffs appear to be plate glass.
They glide sheer into the green immensity,
bow at the base as if they slowly flow

back down into a molten, magma sea.
Right now they mirror the salt-cloud of the sky,
the breathing ocean and the boat's paintwork

lending us the anonymity of rock.
We tack out of the lee onto a high sea,
heading for Barra, tilting through 90 degrees.

We do not recognise ourselves ashore.
Much changed since this morning, we clasp
tea in our grateful hands, the café listing

dangerously. We are still out there with the sharks,
dwarfed by the buckled ramparts' banded gneiss,
the oldest rocks, which melt in front of us.

Later, long since berthed on land, our spirits
tug against the moorings of our bodies,
hear the gannets call us as they pass.

Larina

In that in-between state
not waking nor asleep
but on a sandy strand,
a corridor between
the several worlds
where we have walked
I heard you call my name.

And when I fully woke
I still heard your voice
repeating it, a tinny
word that had been left
in my mind if not my ear
by your urgent call
importing something strange.

But I was not awake
because for many hours
I was alone on that shore
where there was no sea
wondering whether to wake,
what else was in your voice
and what it meant for me.

Royal Sand Pilot

for Paul Farley

I had imagined a lean old man with a staff
leading a few in single file across
an ebbed flat, cut by rivers banked with folds
of wobbling mud, pausing to take soundings
at every tenth step or throwing bolts to test
for sink on each side of the chosen path,

not this biblical multitude who walk
towards the sea in their hundreds on firm sand
or wade the knee-deep Kent with confidence
below the grainy wind, the widest sky.

One day, we will have left these same sands,
the gold, untrammelled sands that are without
footprint under a wilderness of blue,
while water cleans itself as it will do.

A Man

All suthering, ay, in sallows blea.
He clumpsing on across the fen,
by stulp and brig is nestward bound
and ever here by the corner turn,
leaning against that witchens tree,
sees starnels shaping on the wind.

A clouted figure of the ground
who ups from ditches or from woods,
trepid with jolling, rushcap crowned,
the finches flocking round his head,
as if rough chipped from background knap,
from twigs and brambles, crankled brook,
by shocks and stowks: the lonely peep
that nods above the open book.

Elemental

for Penny Redwood

I picture you holding the body, chatting to it,
telling it things you wanted him to know
in the strip-lit side room with its hygiene smell,
once everyone else had gone-out-to-the-car –
how you could yet feel the warmth in his back
exhaling like a sun-warmed wall at night –
and I figure you still have the finger-prints on you
of that other world we never view, the glamour

the dead possess, their out-of-reachness in
the kind of glow that can't be felt or found
through any common sense. This conversation
happened nowhere and cannot be proved,
somewhere between the here and the beyond,
where cold makes us doubt that we are loved.

The Old Camel

In its dotage the Camel forgets
the milky liquid of its dreams
to shuffle between pebble banks.

Where are the level seas of sand
and silver, watery horizon?
It starts to wander through the flags

and reeds as if it has lost
its track in the old station yards
where ghost winds dance. Too late

to run, it spends its final mile
in indecision when it feels
ahead the cloudy terminus of salt.

Local God

Britain assembles as a continent,
volcanoes vent
and mountains grow to Alp-height,
glow a moment, and then wash away
to nothing in the night
leaving behind their red deltas
which will be mountains too one day.

Here, I can feel it everywhere, its quiet
presence felt
in unrelated shapes, the melt
of solifluxion dripping to
a boggy place,
the soil and all that thrives on it,
a shy crag that reveals its face.

You who are hidden by the roadside thorn,
who holds our town,
supports our graveyards and our homes,
you are a kind of prayer we live
inside, that gives
solidity in rain, protects from storms,
yet blows away as dust in air.

You've been around for half a billion years
and calm our fears
by giving ground to tread upon,
a kind of exoskeleton

to bear our weight,
an infrastructure that contains our thought,
a hidden strength to lean against.

God without a name whom none can see,
look out for me
above the soup-thick magma sea,
and in between the lava's fuss
of fumeroles and fire,
be what you are,
be what is underlying us.

Zero Sugar Dream

My pillow's wet where I have dribbled on it.
All of the pictures in my head warn
of the thousand wrecks I made of caravans
and tanker trucks, their metal jagged, torn
and blown-out from within, a silver car-

park full of twisted body-work and sheets
of broken steel. I wander round the site,
a shiny sense of needing something sweet
flapping about in the corner like a length
of crime-scene tape toyed with by the wind.

Inside a tanker shell, a ruined home
has been laid bare, all of the calm and in-
door artefacts ripped up and strewn about,
the children stunned, as if a terraced street
had been swept by a vast tornado snout.

And there it is, beyond the wrecked machines,
hoovering the plough, the funnel cloud
a blind, prosthetic and prehensile nose
that sweeps the landscape looking for its prey,
its swollen body full of spinning dolls.

Appalled that it was me imagined this,
I see the black trunk pause and start to scout
the ground as if it was intelligent,
its vengeful, pursuing limb lock on to me . . .
I stumble as I feed myself awake.

Neolithic

For years it glowed in the dark,
a slim green axe of stone
behind the cabinet glass,
its inlaid mottle skin
centuries-smooth with use.

To me, it showed a new
species of discovery,
where stone was malleable
and could be made to bend
its rigour to intent,

the kind of dawning that makes
your eyes bleach and the world
go black, although the lore
of the lesson will still take
aeons to implement.

I couldn't pass it without
a shiver as if some sliver
of me recognised that dark
is long, that all things are
exchangeable, the way

our atoms touch and move
apart, the patterns the ages
make, the shadows walking
down millennia
and all that dark ahead.

Ballad of Berber Time

This morning, as the charcoal rain
falls on the soot-black streets,
I feel time sing a new refrain,
pass to a different beat.

It's Berber Time, a place where things
move in a different way,
where the sound of nothing happening
deafens me every day;

where time is empty, nothing occurs
and there are no events;
no time passes, nothing stirs,
not even grass is bent;

or else the days are full of things,
so rich in time as well,
the busy day well-fed; it sings
and as it sings it swells.

Theirs is a magic clock where hours
are counted differently,
where time puts on a servant's powers
and brings me cake and tea.

I dawdle with a vacant mind
and open what it brings:
light-flakes, some seeds of grow-the-wind,
a throw of bright nothings.

These are my raw materials
that I stretch out or shrink,
distil into a cordial
that I dilute and drink.

This elasticity of time
is one of the Berber arts,
they don't divide the one sublime
with a clock of equal parts.

But now there's so much less of it,
time flies and I speed too
towards the dark of death, in transit
to a place-time that's taboo.

II

Black Box

The Original Influencing Machine (1706)

to Francis Hauksbee

I place my hands as gently as I can
around the globe that glows below my skin
and a magic lantern of coronal wind
passes through my skull to touch my mind.
I watch the pictures form out of thin air
as shadows walk and breathe inside the sphere.
I feel the static build as currents swim
and watch my thoughts like dancing cherubim.

A grating noise: I drag the globe across
the stone floor of my den. Inside the room
its astral light illuminates the chaos
of this cluttered life. Despite the gloom
I see things clearly now: inside the ball,
the room. All life is electrical.

The Air-Loom (1797)

to James Tilley Matthews

machine, v.: to contrive, plot (against a person)

A thousand operators come and go
in hugger-mugger to this secret rite
and carefully avert their eyes in case
they spot each other in the faint twilight,
the intricate machine they stand beside –
all copper tubes and bobbins ringed with brass,
distilling thoughts like thread out of thin air –

an instrument of what will come to pass.
The woven thoughts are fired across the street
and sown in minds as dreams begin their light-
show in the brain, becoming part of what
we think is ours, as close as air at night
creeps to our blood, more intimate than touch.
Although the feather breath that brushes you

with its miasmal stealth is not your breath,
you cannot tell it from your own and, though
inside you and not of you, you won't know.
Next day you find unfathomable thoughts
tucked like bookmarks in between your own,
surprised at knowing things you were not taught.
I've seen these men as they pursue their ends

with grim intrigue and fear what they believe,
have heard about caprices such as theirs
and watched them warp the world into their weave.
When they are done and all their thoughts reside
in heads that steer the foundering ship of state,
they pack away the hardware, slip outside
onto the street and then evaporate.

The Afterlife of the Air-Loom (1919)

to Viktor Tausk

When it had spun its thoughts and left for dead
the poor man in his cell of abscesses,
the ghost machine evolved, became a box
of tricks, all micro-waves and mobile masts,
a soup of circuitry from which it wove
all of the dreams of Man, the vital parts
a baby body cannot fathom out.

A black Ur-box, it sits now on my desk,
a panel on the front, a toggle, wires
entering a sealed socket at the back.
Thus the mind presents the body: as
a nebula of darkness, infinite
inside but small and definite in size.
It hums the hymn of electricity.

If I contained it in another box
and buried it in darkness down below
and sealed them all inside the deepest mine
I could not stop it uttering its thoughts.
Though blank and dangerous, it condescends
to let the mind envisage it and works
its wonders by itself, for its own ends.

How Operators Make You Do (1958)

to Barbara O'Brien

The box is everything – inside its cool
jet surface, something stirs. My smallest thought
is taken by its wavy lines that wash
into my skull and scoop my brain out:
the myth of perfect, svelte machinery
that fires inside a sealed exterior
and makes of me an oiled, hypnotic slave.

The box is magnet, gun and so much more –
it shoots exploding words into my head
and serves them up on plates as word salad.
It pulls the sentences out of my mouth
as I speak them. I'm porous. When it pours
I fill with rain and, as the box decides,
I reach my tipping point and rain myself.

Remote Surveillance (2017)

It all comes down to us, eventually:
miasma segues into smog, then Clean
Air Acts while radiation reaches out
its wavelengths for impressionable minds.
Our fear is always on the move, switching
between stations, on the look-out for a signal,
those metal ears that turn as the world turns.

We sit at consoles, monitor the screens,
imagining the masters – sat in gantries
quartering the Earth, the data streams,
the market oscillations – keeping tabs
on everything that moves. Neutrino beams
seek out our drop-zones, fumble for a thought
and slip it softly through the letterbox.

A false self camped inside each sleeping brain,
Manchurian candidates who dream of power,
fifth columnists inside a conquered self,
Helsinki syndrome separatists who signed
for someone else the future of us all;
the dreams we dream in sleep laboratories,
that great suggestions box, the human mind.

III
Desolate Market

The Slug Autumn

I was all of a spin like the lime-keys
on their hesitant descent: they'd rise
as if seeking their first height
when they were cradled by the breeze,
twizzling faster as though this surfeit
of air had made them improvise.

I'd been let go: suddenly nothing
expected me, the phone silent, left
out of the general tide, becalmed
but not content. I awaited its ring,
I sat on my own as if adrift
on my own current, hurt but unharmed,

the whispering behind my back
had stopped although I still heard
voices talking me down. They'd snarl
and snigger, stating their plan of attack.
They had invaded me. I feared
I was fraying like old material.

Pale and luminescent slugs
were feeding on each other, their mouths
sunk in each other's black, slick skin.
Their crushed bodies clogged our rugs,
the ground was alive with them, our clothes
crawled with their shell-less slithering.

A thin rain wets the slime.
I watch the slugs at their commerce,
the way an enemy might.
Everything happens a trillion times
in the huge hangar of the universe;
and nothing ever comes out right.

Care

This word is a stoped-out lode: look at the slag
that petticoats the hillside where we stand. It falls
in screes like fantails from the adit's mouth (a hole
that gapes in a toothless, uninquiring way), a rag

of spoil against the limestone dale. Care
is full of rusty pools where the seep of oil has turned
the pit-floor to a rainbow sump; machines abandoned,
dropped by the men who worked the seams bare

and died, their lives as unremembered as the earth,
their toils unappreciated. Many years passed
before an overseer was appointed, then at best
he counted only the pigs, inscribing their worth.

The word itself still stands, hollow, ill-used.
They were planning a museum in it, but staff
have been laid off and cobwebs handkerchief
the corners where a glint of kindness is accused.

Morrigan

She is everywhere: terror flaps awry
from blood-soaked fields, its primaries wet red.
There are enough of her to mystify

the panicked men (their wits loose in their heads),
to funnel them through birches, gorse and heather
to plateaux where they shiver, left for dead

in foul fields where they grow their own feathers
that cannot help them fly but keep them warm
at least, a cloudy cloak for every weather.

She harries them so they will come to harm,
each now alone in fog and fen among
unfriendly farms, with no sweet marjoram.

These madmen wander in the woods so long,
misled by soft words whispered in their ears,
they can't tell bad from good or right from wrong

and she's been busy in more recent years,
vacuuming minds she wants to hypnotise
and filling them with excrement and fears.

She hides in plain view now, needs no disguise.
We cannot tell her from our own and wait,
all innocence, while falling for her lies.

Her voice is sleep-inducing, laced with hate.
What would happen if her trap was sprung?
We wouldn't know until it was too late.

Her pleasure is to wash her hands in young
men's blood, to suck their wounds' lips, snap their bones,
invade their minds to make them come unstrung

and ready to possess, stockpiling guns
and searching for lost souls to foist them on,
or giving them away with mobile phones.

She lurks in gaps, a blank phenomenon
but only has to look them in the eye
and they're already hers and are half-gone.

A Separation

A bright blade of moon melting
in its own black wax, a ball
bearing in a silver pool, a shield
mirroring sun and space,
a rocker at full rock.

I can see where Blake rested his ladder,
on that horn parallel to the horizon,
and feel a similar pull towards
this arch companion that inch
by inch at one-point-five per year

is drifting away from us.
The tides are trying to hold
on, exerting their own sway
over the wan globe, rising
above their own horizon,

that moves them less each day.
Tonight the old moon sits
in its rocking chair, unlit
as a dead bulb, to feel the slow
sadness of letting go.

The Rhubarb Triangle

for Ian Duhig

In a frost pocket behind the Pennine chain
where water, slack and shoddy can be found
the Tusky Fields expose their pale fangs,
grow rich in red and green and sprout again,
while children huddle on the broken ground
or creep into the twilit forcing sheds.
Keep warm by candlelight, O boys and girls,
where vegetables that held the price of pearls,
as valuable as opium and rare as love,
begin the dim-lit, slow unfolding of
their poisonous leaves. In this depleted zone
the seeds of darkness crop as wan-faced kids
are harvested and flee to London on
the Rhubarb Trains or disappear in Leeds.

These Are Our Toys

We are like enormous children at a party:
our legs won't fit under the table and no one
seems to know the rules of the game, so we always
end up arguing and going off into corners to sulk.
The jelly hasn't set properly and the adults are dead.

The twins have been to the bathroom and broken a tap
and now water is coming down the stairs. A voice sounds
from a speaker on the wall and says we have all been bad,
very bad. Some of us start to cry and say *it wasn't me.*

The television has been confiscated and pocket money
withdrawn for an unspecified length of time.
We still have our toys – the belief that we are important,
that someone is looking after us and that if we behave
we will be rewarded – and they have consoled us

up until now, but one or two of us have begun
to ask if they work any more. I'm feeling
poorly and must have done something really bad
because I can hear the click of approaching heels.

Smoke and Mirrors

from The Arcades Project

He texts me saying 'everything is bright,
the morning sun sets sparkle to the glass,
the stock stands forward in a pool of light,
I wow my mistresses all through the night
and markets climb, all good things come to pass.'

I picture his emporium: light pours
through ceiling panes and makes the inside seem
eternal, multiplied and spread by mirrors
that extend the shop beyond its walls, extreme
assertiveness that pushes through its doors

and cannot satisfy itself. It eats
through every boundary, each one deprived
of all significance, as light deletes
the shadow-space we need to live and thrive in
unobserved, like doorstoppers on the streets,

or cold-callers in our homes. The glare goes on;
it flattens space and permeates all fields,
despite their innocence, and takes our children
from our sides, seducing us again
with the brilliance of a sudden leg, revealed

beneath a lifted skirt. There is no point
in trying to hide: such light leaks everywhere,
illuminates the grit that wrecks each joint,
the highlights she has scattered in her hair,
a light that always has to disappoint.

The whispering of gazes fills the arcades.
We have abandoned virtue for a view
that looks both ways the better to parade
the *fantastical magnitude* of all our new
commodities. And there is only trade

to fill the world with and those things we hate
about ourselves and cannot tolerate
we sell so easily to other folk
and when they buy them give it to them straight:
an everyday and savage kind of joke.

But up and down have ceased to make much sense,
there is confusion at each compass point.
The Invisible Committee planned these events,
the ones who leave no audit trail, who spent
our cash before it entered our account,

whose cover is so deep they can't be seen,
the ones the agents of the State protect.
The old conspiracies, like kerosene,
were dangerous if left to burn unchecked;
our new ones, glossy with chimera-sheen,

are snide, impossible to penetrate,
so insubstantial no one thinks they're real
although their impacts are as great.
We victims, who are left without appeal,
wander amid the drifting smoke or wait

for justice which will never come. We burn
the larder of the Earth to stock our store
as we wait for the *inevitable* upturn.
We sit cross-legged like deserving poor.
We let the light illuminate. We yearn.

Baul of Bengal

Here the bits of glass can catch the sun,
here no one casts their shadow over you,
here the dust is shaped by the ghost wind,
a place for the passed-over and condemned.

Unfit for leadership, self management
or profit-drive, even to sell myself,
I sit here singing in my patchwork coat
with nothing in my *jhola* or my throat

and with this nothing, sing and thrive. The love-
bazaar around me is my wealth. I re-
possess what others throw away, my part
to know the *maner manus* of my heart,

the one who sits inside my skull below
the thousand-petalled lotus and descends
to meet the woman and become complete.
My skin and bone turn gold where rivers meet

as she and I are joined. I only need
to squat here in the sun to be made one
among the broken glass, my sun-struck jewels;
I hold the one-stringed instrument of fools.

Whereof We Cannot Speak

Extreme harm takes the house by storm.
My daughter cannot sleep.
I hear the undercurrents form
that run too deep
but, fed on solitude for fuel,
I have to double lock the gloom
to keep the infinitely cruel
out of our living room.

How many shadows are there, massed
beyond the firelight,
how many fears from the past
plague us at night?
They loom above our innocent
concerns and drain the goodness out,
they haunt us with a scent,
prey on our doubt.

You taught me shadows, how they harm
and how to live with them;
you took me to the poisoned farm
for nature's requiem,
the boils erupting from the ground,
the stinking fumeroles
and cess-pits where we found
the pyres of souls.

Too much for me. My mind unzipped
itself, and spilled my ink
in squirts into a manuscript

no one could read.
It was impossible to think:
I wore my fears like medals, proud,
while others heard me bleed
out loud.

A cat curled up against a pane,
a wet face left behind,
the tail-lights of departing trains
gone from the mind:
the shadows land like burns across
my shoulders, as I walk
between unnumbered lonelinesses
hugged by the dark.

Dream City

from *The Arcades Project*

Your head close-shaved by some barbarian
to ease the paddles' contact with the scalp,
still sly, your sideways glance civilian,
so rich in ironies. And ask for help?
You'd never in a hundred years, a million.

Instead your brain, that precious instrument,
recorded everything, helped you escape
through gothic passageways where no one went,
down trap-doors through the strata; you would wipe
each memory, even if it was innocent.

That was your gift – to always get away
from whoever or whatever chased you down,
forgetting what had held you in its sway;
move house, ditch friends or disconnect the phone
and you'd finesse the rest. A bit blasé

about the past, soon you would be awake
and then what terrible beasts would come to be,
what eldritch shapes would your experience take,
what creatures looming that you could not see
straight out of darkness? Because we are opaque.

The fact becomes a thing that just now, first,
is happening: we'd all be blinded by
the truth if all we'd lived through in a burst
revealed itself, but strapped against the sky
you were irradiated by the worst

and yet you held each Roentgen memory
to let it work its ministry of fear,
enslaved by each page of your diary,
each new shame piercing you, a sharp spear
of pain from echoes buried in your body.

The work was endless, balanced on an edge
each moment as you took another breath
and helping you to live a privilege
because I carried pictures of your death
around with me each day: you on the ledge

waiting to drop, incarnadining your bath,
going down to darkness drowned in pills
or murdered by some two-bit psychopath,
each flash of memory adding to your ills,
the dream of peace barely a future myth.

For you, awaking was like being flayed
as if you had to tear each layer off,
each lie you had to loosen with a blade
until you had it on a polygraph
and could interrogate it with a spade.

And after all of that, we're in the copse
of lethargies frustrated, poorly, still.
The Great Common Ground between us drops
away, the city moves in for the kill,
its slumbers painting masks for agitprop,

and adverts try to sell us what they want,
a vast dream of a dream of waking up.
The curtains sway, aurora-like, their drop
illusory and incomplete, a front
we cannot get behind, a tease, a prop.

We struggle to remember even this:
the basics of our lives, who loved us, where
we lived, our homes and what remains of us.
In this city of the darkest ruins, here
we will make a stand, here we will undress,

reveal ourselves as flaws in data streams
to those who want us to remain asleep.
Nothing is ever only what it seems.
The stations are the factories of dreams
and what we want is buried just too deep.

The Hook

I may no longer be held to account
for that person's fear of leaves
because I threw a torn-up scatter
of paper at them as they cried
when they were young.

And yet I cannot look into my child's
heart and see the fear that grows
like a large tree, ring on ring
as the years expand their girth
and leaves yellow and fall.

Regret is a sweet word. I can
not utter it at all and know
what manner of sorrow and shame
may visit me. I feel a weight
of blossom big as space.

Recovery Room

Light struggles through the palsied glass where, pale
and bespoke, the colours of disease disguise
our faces, worming into pores: it is
a myth, that we who are not sick are hale.
I'm only waiting for my illnesses
to show mysteriously like eggs of flies.

The whole edifice hums, as if a current ran
through every floor, connecting up each ward
and linking thoughts like neurones in a brain
where every part knows everything. No doubt
my fear comes from below the ground where gaudy
theatres glow. They tore your insides out

and wheeled you back to idle in the light.
Your body's here, your pale face on your gown
but you are in the shallows of the night.
This is the great machine that makes the dark
in a sealed and unobtrusive room. I walk
with you not knowing which way you will turn.

Translation

Take school. There isn't one that doesn't smell
of wet cloths, cabbage, custard slopped from cans,
   of being forced to eat by matrons
who have ladles where they should have hands.

It's better to forget those *best days of*.
The bully shadowed you. You ran from him
   to trysting places where he took
whole fists of you in his beside the gym.

You never knew enough, as though a sea
unknown and vast was weighing on your desk,
   a foreign language chilling you
with cold tons of questions you couldn't ask.

Such details changed you and you lost your light
that faded like a rainbow starved of sun,
   all colours shamed by words which stung:
a bit of application gets things done.

Now, every day you take your kids to school
and watch their eyes swim as you say goodbye;
   setting them the same unseens.
You walk away not knowing how, or why.

IV
Silent Vacuum

Likely Story

The six-times veteran of shuttle trips
you watch afloat in space on NASA footage
in a bright-white Michelin-Man suit, a jet
black hole exactly where his face should be,
Story Musgrave talks a good alien.
The billion-coloured stars in his visor swim
two hundred miles above a midnight ocean,
while we're marooned on Earth, the listening ears
of telescopes that turn like cups to catch
dark matter distillate condensed from stars
and all those pretty wishes humans launch
in hope but which come dripping back to earth

like spent desire. We can't concede as much,
despite our noise, and poke and probe the space
beyond what we can reach by unmanned flight
with spectral instruments that feel for us
in each cramped corner of the infinite.
Up there I've felt their presences, he says.
I heard them waiting watching wanting us
to know another darkness in the dark.
And Story put the Hubble there himself,
he heard the ripples spread by the Big Bang,
he has in mind dimensions without end
that lie behind his space-black, star-lit face.

The Big Beasts

When Jupiter began its grand trek in
from the ice of outer space where giants grow
towards our star's inimitable heat,
there were results: its great bulk threw a mass
of rock and ice into the mouth of the sun,
tribute from one big beast to another.

It ate up the solar disc, it swallowed whole
planets, debris about to become super-Earths,
and cleared broad swathes of swirling dust and gas,
it ate the inner proto-planets, a space-
tornado hoovering residual mass,
building itself until it almost shone.

When this near-star had finished up its feast
Mars became a tenth the mass of Earth.
So little value and renown were left
it could not hold onto its atmosphere
and, were it not a neighbour to ourselves,
no one would regard it in the least.

Asteroid Hyalosis

Alone and hung between infinities
of space and those enormous empty rooms
inside the micro-worlds of things we see
(that solid-looking stuff that comforts us),
we seem so utterly insignificant
our measure should be the Planck length, a hundred
billion, billion times smaller than a quark.

And these opacities that cloud my sight
like flakes of paint inside a paperweight
are flaws that mimic universal laws
so when I close my eyes against the light
I see their constellations of dark stars
picked out against my lids, my very own
heavens comprising a few fragments of bone.

Lurking in the depths of the Oort Cloud
the dormant proto-comets and their like
beyond the Kuiper Belt, the planetismals,
centaurs, asteroids and dwarf planets,
Trojans, satellites with their own satellites,
and thousands more discovered every year,
a mass of bodies orbits round the sun.

Not so alone then, as I lie and watch
them drift across the space between myself
and what's out there; a mesh of moving shapes,
irregular and spindly Voyagers
rotating as all bodies do in space,
in that silent vacuum that separates,
the depths in everyone that can't be read.

They are a kind of comfort, in the way
illusions are: my Hilda Family
of specks and wires that move as my eyes move,
companions that travel with me where I go.
They're so pretty, she says, scrying the depths
of my eye with a white light. They glitter sparely,
turning in the beam like strips of Window.

NOTES

Hilda Family: a dynamical group of asteroids in a 3:2 orbital
    resonance with Jupiter.
Window: The English term for Chaff, shredded tin-foil dropped
    from bombers that was used to create radar blindness in
    WW2 through which they could fly unscathed.

The Fountain

I saw it once before, when I was young
and still unsettled in the world, a spin
of thought and things that poured out as a spring.
I'd woken up to find the origin
and watched it start to spill out bursts
of forests, hills and plants with violet tongues
for leaves, horseheads of gas like knobs of karst,
the nursery grounds of fuzzy stars, their lungs
igniting dust.
        And it was she who showed
it me – Larina who appeared inside
and steered me here by this neglected road,
who stayed with me and asked to be my guide.

Dusk's colours, crimson lake and indigo
in clouds of light and ice collected round
the fountain in a rapidly rotating halo
that spun forever and without a sound
as every solid or imagined thing
flew into being from the cloaking cloud
and every object with its own note sang
in frightened silence as it stood out proud
against the backdrop of the universe.
Creation was a cold and lonely art,
shadows of red-shift darkening its source.

All of space was tense with expectancy:
burning boulders crashed into the heart
of the spinning globe, molten fire cascading
from the origin to knit roots for the world tree,

the knot that ties the inner core onto
the streaming heights of atmosphere, the birth
of rock that anchors minute worlds of dew
to leaves. White gold of magma laced the Earth.

I stood and watched the sweet debris emerge
from matter's whirlpools on the mats of time,
their each dent different. I saw the patterns
as they came and changed, the paradigms
of space and thought, the architectural plans
for life, the shape of each molecular bond
and understood its own specific strength,
perceived the size and limits of the mind
and with a calliper's precision the length
between the smallest part and the most great.

I thought the fragile rock-lip where I stood
endangered by a fast-approaching threat
because a mortal watched the works of God.
That fear, though, was another sort, the kind
that makes us feel so small we might die, out
of insignificance or lose our mind
because our frailty is so absolute.

And now, unasked for, I am given a sight
of this great fountain in my later years:
although I'm old, I see what I forgot
as scales fall from my eyes and all is clear:
not sick, nor poisoned by illusion's forms,
nor cloyed by sentiment, the fountain speaks
in silence to my inner, swirling storms.
Stripped of importance, I am at least awake –
I know I have been torn from something whole,

lost parts of me split off from which I run
alone, apart, adrift, cut off from all
I want to be and know I never can.

Torn from eternity at break of day
I see her as I first imagined her,
with seagull hair wet with Atlantic spray,
treading the ancient rock of Eigneig Mhor,
her pacing shape at night against the glow
of phosphorescent waves so solitary.

I raise my head and watch the fountain flow,
its currents knotting up loose ends in me,
dwarfed by this huge, disinterested machine
spinning its great designs of flesh and soul,
dizzy enough to die as, in between,
each night-sky sighting of her takes its toll.

Hard Rain

for Lottie Williams, patron saint of orbital debris

The dead persist as junk in orbit round
the mind, their planet-weight of space-waste cold
from years of disregard, and sometimes land:
watch for the tracer as they fall, the golden
rain of burn-up in the air, the charcoaled
lumps of sky-iron lying on the sand.

Think about all that stuff spinning there,
the derelict craft, flecks of paint, shrapnel
from missile tests, spanners and other hardware
dropped on space-walks; all those who dwell
in deep space, orbiting this place, beware
of how we can be utterly forgetful.

The dead's detritus passes through the mind
when we are idly staring into space
or driving home from being entertained:
a flash of meteor might scratch a trace
on the cornea that fades but leaves behind
surprise and something wet wiped from the face.